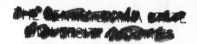

Radio-Assisted Community Basic Education

DOMINICAN REPUBLIC

- International boundary
- ⊛ National capital
- ┼┼┼ Railroad
- Road
- ✛ International airport

0 20 40 Miles
0 20 40 Kilometers

ATLANTIC OCEAN

CARIBBEAN SEA

HAITI

Monte Cristi
Pepillo
Salcedo
Cap-Haitien
Fort
Liberté
Gonaïves
Rivière Artibonite
PORT-
AU-PRINCE

Río Yaque del Norte
Dajabón
Sabaneta
Mao
Santiago
Luperón
Puerto
Plata
Cabrera
Nagua
Gaspar
Hernández
San Francisco
de Macorís
Moca
Salcedo
La
Vega
Rincón
Cotuí
Bonao
Río Yuna
Camú

Sánchez
Samaná
Sabana de La Mar
Miches
El Seibo
Higüey
Boca
de Yuma
ISLA
SAONA
La Romana
San Pedro
de Macorís
SANTO
DOMINGO
Haina
Río Ozama
Río Haina
San
Cristóbal
Baní
Las Calderas

Río
Artibonite
Elías Piña
San Juan
Río Yaque del Sur
Neiba
LAGO
ENRIQUILLO
Jimaní
Barahona
Pedernales
Oviedo
ISLA
BEATA
Azua
Río Ocoa

Radio-Assisted Community Basic Education (RADECO)

United States Agency for International Development

Office of Education, Bureau for Science and Technology.

(Project Editors)
**Ruth Eshgh, James Hoxeng,
Johanna Provenzano and Beatriz Casals**

Duquesne University Press
Pittsburgh, PA

Published in the United States of America in 1988 by

Duquesne University Press
600 Forbes Avenue
Pittsburgh, PA 15282

The RADECO project was funded under Agency for International
Development Contract DPE 5807-C-00-1046-00 with InterAmerica Research
Associates, Inc.

Publication of this document was funded under Agency for International
Development contract DPE 1109-C-00-4081-00 with the Institute for
International Research. Views expressed herein are those of the contributors
and do not necessarily reflect policy of the Agency for International
Development or the United States Government.

Library of Congress Cataloging-in-Publication Data

Radio-assisted community basic education.

1. Radio in education—Dominican Republic—Case Studies. 2. Basic education—
Dominican Republic—Case studies. 3. Education, Rural—Dominican Republic—
Case studies. 4. Educational assistance, American—Dominican Republic—Case
studies. I. Eshgh, Ruth. II. United States. Agency for International Development.
Bureau for Science and Technology. Office of Education.
LB1044.6D65R33 1988   372.13'331'097293   87-32987   .D65R33
ISBN 0-8207-0196-3

Printed in the United States of America

Institute for
World Concerns Series

Contents

List of Figures and Tables

Figures

Tables

Preface

The Radio-Assisted Community Basic Education (RADECO) Project was initiated in Barahona, Dominican Republic, in 1981. The project is one element in the U.S. Agency for International Development's (USAID) long-range plan to help developing countries gain greater access to educational opportunities. This monograph is a synthesis of papers prepared for an international radio conference held in Santa Domingo in December 1985, at which representatives from organizations in Latin America and the United States became acquainted with the RADECO model. The volume describes and explains each major component of the RADECO project. The introduction recounts the role of radio instruction in development education. Chapter one provides an overview of the RADECO model and the concept of interactive radio. Chapter two describes the outreach component, which was responsible for the integration of RADECO into selected communities. Chapter three details the curriculum that was scripted into radio lessons in mathematics and language arts. Chapter four provides insight into the production of the lessons, and Chapter five discusses RADECO's use of both formative and summative evaluation designs to guide the development of lessons and to assess teaching effectiveness. The final two chapters discuss the institutionalization of the project and adaptation of the RADECO model.

The volume is a compendium of papers and research produced by the following RADECO project personnel and consultants, listed with their respective contributions: *Introduction* by James Hoxeng, RADECO Project Officer, USAID; *The RADECO Model* by John F. Helwig, Former Chief of Party, RADECO, and Jamesine Friend, Friend Dialogues, Inc.; *Interactive Radio* by David Edgerton, Chief of Party, RADECO; *Outreach* by Jose Licano Palma, University of Arizona, and Diane de Terra, Consultant; *Curriculum Development* by Jamesine Friend, David Edgerton, and Altagracia Diaz de De Jesus, Technical Coordinator, RADECO; *Production* by Sonia Andujar, Radio Producer, RADECO, and Gilda Rosa, Radio Producer, RADECO; *Evaluation* by Jamesine Friend and Steven Kozlow, Former Technical Coordinator, RADECO; *Institutionalization* by John Helwig and David Edgerton; and *Adaptation of the RADECO Model* by John Helwig, David Edgerton, and Jorge Sanguinetty, DETEC.

Introduction

In general, rural schooling in the Third World is a bleak experience. Mud and wattle walls weaken quickly in the tropical weather; corrugated tin roofs are boilermakers under sunlight and cacophonous in downpours. Windows, if they exist, are small; larger openings would weaken the walls. Dust is everywhere; textbooks are scarce. Rural schools as a rule have fewer teaching materials and employ less-experienced teachers than their urban counterparts. Many rural teachers are new graduates who are required to spend a year or two in remote areas before they can return to the urban areas where they grew up.

This environment is the challenge facing development educators: the poorest settings have the least experienced instructors and the most rudimentary support. When radio and television were first considered as means of meeting this challenge, there was high optimism that quantum changes would follow immediately. Not so. Television has all but disappeared from Third World education plans. Radio, however, has shown enough promise to spur continued adaptation and testing.

As their cost has decreased, radios have become standard items in poor households. While batteries are still expensive, people somehow find the money to purchase them. At the same time, broadcasting capacity has grown

remarkably. Radio broadcasts can now be heard throughout the Third World.

INITIAL RADIO EDUCATION PROJECTS

The first and in many ways still the flagship radio education program is Acción Cultural Popular (ACPO) in
Colombia. The ACPO basic education course is a four-
month program providing daily thirty-minute broadcasts
designed to provide basic literacy skills. Adults and children alike meet in the home of one of the students to listen.
A volunteer monitor—often a former ACPO student—helps
students with specific problems. Rural libraries and a weekly
newspaper provide information and reinforce learning.

From humble beginnings in 1947, in the small mountain
village of Sutatenza, ACPO radiophonics schools have now
been extended to every corner of the country. Programming has broadened to deliver instruction to rural Colom-
bians in virtually all subjects. ACPO's example has been
followed throughout Latin America.

Another important radio education initiative was the
USAID program begun in Nicaragua in 1974. Originated
by Stanford University, in cooperation with the Ministry
of Education, this five-year project differed from the APCO
model in three major ways. First, instead of using radio
to set up new schools, the project brought radio into existing classrooms. Second, radio was used for only one
subject, mathematics, which preliminary investigation had
shown was the most difficult subject for primary teachers
and assistance in guiding students through the curriculum
would be welcomed. Third, Nicaragua Radio Mathematics
introduced an interactive style of teaching, which involved
a much greater number of radio-student questions and

responses than the radiophonic model. In contrast to the traditional ACPO model, where considerable time was allotted for instructions by the radio teacher, Radio Math called for out-loud student responses two or three times a minute. Immediate reinforcement was provided by giving the correct answer after every student response, and musical cues were used to signal the next activity. The room was noisy, but the students were almost constantly fully engaged.

Following the success of the Nicaraguan project in improving student performance, the interactive model was adapted for reading and language arts in a USAID project carried out by the Academy for Educational Development in Kenya from 1980 to 1985. There radio instruction was offered in rural classrooms with the aim of teaching English to children in the first three grades. Evaluation found significant gains in speaking, listening, and reading skills, and a very high level of satisfaction on the part of teachers and parents as well as students.

As the final phase of the USAID radio education initiative, a new project to adapt the model for science began in 1986. In Papua New Guinea, the Education Development Center has responsibility for applying the interactive approach to deliver science education to a wide spectrum of classrooms across that country's difficult terrain.

THE RADECO PROJECT

How does the Radio-Assisted Community Basic Education project (RADECO) fit into the model used in Nicaragua, Kenya, and Papua New Guinea? RADECO combines key elements of the radiophonic model and interactive radio into its own unique approach. Like ACPO and its followers, RADECO created learning centers where there were no schools or teachers. Its initial emphasis was on increasing access rather than on improving the quality of existing instruction. However, RADECO drew directly on the interactive approach of the USAID projects to adapt the Dominican Republic's curriculum to radio. RADECO classes look and sound very much like project classrooms in Nicaragua and Kenya.

The agreement signed between the governments of the Dominican Republic and the United States had three main objectives:

• To develop an effective teaching program at low cost for school-age children. The program was to be based on the national curriculum, tailored to the nation's history and culture, and delivered by radio.

• To adapt classes for grades one through four for delivery by radio, with formal certification for students successfully completing each year.

• To train Dominicans in all techniques and skills needed to carry out the program.

In short, RADECO is a hybrid, drawing on the strengths of both major radio education strains. People from the radiophonics tradition find much to interest them in RADECO, as do educators for whom radio is a completely new instructional medium. A number of countries are now considering yet another variation—using radio for several subjects in existing schools to help inexperienced teachers. The possibilities are intriguing.

1/The RADECO Model

From daybreak until the afternoon, the children of Cortico, Arriba, Camboya, and Algodon pick coffee, carry water, shine shoes, haul garbage, and cut and carry sugar cane. These children do not go to school. They are too busy during the day, and many cannot afford the necessary uniforms or supplies required for school attendance. The overall enrollment rate in the primary grades in the Dominican Republic is reported to be 91 percent. In the remote southwestern region of the Dominican Republic, however, one-fifth of the primary-school-age children are not enrolled in schools; most of these are in rural areas. Many communities do not even have schools or teachers.

That was the situation prior to January 24, 1983, the date that Radio-Assisted Community Basic Education (RADECO) went on the air. Now, after their work is done, the children assemble at a RADECO learning center where they are greeted by an adult paraprofessional proctor called a radioauxiliary. The radioauxiliary distributes clipboards and work sheets, and the students settle into their places. Just before four o'clock, a battery-powered radio is switched on and tuned to the RADECO hour—an hour of systematic instruction in reading, writing, mathematics, music, games, and physical exercises.

Unlike other radio education projects that have attempted to improve in-school instruction in one specific

1

subject area within a formal school setting, RADECO's objectives are to provide a comprehensive basic education through an intensive, innovative interactive educational program where no formal schools are available. Each RADECO grade level consists of 170 one-hour lessons divided approximately into twenty-five minutes of mathematics, twenty-five minutes of language, and ten minutes of social science, natural science, and recreation segments. At the end of each grade, RADECO students are expected to have acquired the equivalent basic education of their peers in the regular public schools in the region.

RADECO provides cost-effective, accessible schooling for a population that has no other avenue to obtain it. Rather than teachers, members of the community who can read and write are selected to convene the classes and direct the students in following the radio lessons. The "schools" are modest shelters or *enramadas* that are erected by each recipient community. Community and family costs of participation in the project are negligible. There are neither expensive textbooks nor school uniforms to buy; instructional materials are mimeographed work sheets to be used with the radio lessons.

CONTEXT OF THE RADECO PROJECT

The Dominican Republic constitutes 74 percent of the island of Hispaniola, which is at the center of the Antilles; Haiti comprises the other 26 percent. RADECO was implemented in the province of Barahona (see map, page 00), in the southwestern region of the country near the Haitian border. Barahona, the southwest province, includes approximately 25 percent of the land and 15 percent of the Dominican Republic's six million citizens. The province's population is widely dispersed, and its communities are small; most have no organized government.

The southwest is the poorest region in the country. The highest indices of infant mortality and malnutrition are found there, along with the highest rates of illiteracy. Family incomes are low, housing is substandard. The communities working with the RADECO project are mostly in coffee-growing regions or on sugar cane plantations; some are in fishing communities or subsistence farming areas; a few are located on the outskirts of larger towns.

Typical RADECO students are rural and work in the fields alongside their parents. When asked why they wanted their children to be educated, parents give varied answers: "I want my children to learn so I will not be cheated at the store or when my harvest is weighed . . . so they can read farm bulletins to me and I can improve crops." "So they can read directions for medicine." "So they can get jobs, eat, get ahead in life." These parents see the education of their children as a means of improving the living conditions of the entire family.

PROGRAM GOVERNANCE

Four organizations collaborated in administering the RADECO project: USAID/Washington's Bureau for Science and Technology; the USAID Mission in the Dominican Republic; the Dominican Secretariat of Education, Fine Arts, and Religion (SEEBAC); and InterAmerica Research Associates under contract to USAID.

The USAID Office of Education in the Bureau for Science and Technology in Washington, D.C., was responsible for designing, developing, funding, and monitoring the project. The USAID Mission in the Dominican Republic provided technical and logistical support and carried major responsibility for day-to-day project assistance. SEEBAC, which was responsible for authorizing and supervising all educational enterprises and programs at primary and secondary levels in the Dominican Republic, supplied most of the project staff. Acquisition and provision of air time was also SEEBAC's responsibility. InterAmerica was responsible for the financial management of the project and for providing technical assistance in the form of long-term field staff, short-term consultancies, and subcontracts. The project called for the InterAmerica team to work directly with seconded SEEBAC staff and other Dominican personnel during the initial stages of the project, training them to write scripts, produce radio lessons, evaluate the lessons, and supervise the schools.

From the beginning RADECO was intended to become a permanent part of SEEBAC's program. The project agreement stated, "It is expected that by the end of the project, SEEBAC staff, as a result of on-the-job training and in-country workshops, will assume the responsibility of designing and disseminating additional radio education programs for primary school students between the ages of 7 to 14 years."

At an early stage of project implementation a Coordination and Review Committee (CRC) was established to serve as an advisory board. The CRC, chaired by the Secretary of Education or a sub-secretary, was charged with determining and interpreting project policies and with recommending solutions for problems regarding personnel, logistics, and support. The CRC was comprised of SEEBAC Directors of Educational Media, Curriculum, Primary Education, and Training; InterAmerica's Chief of Party; RADECO's Executive Director; and a representative of USAID. The CRC also nominally included representatives of the Southwest Development Authority (INDESUR) and the National Planning Office (ONAPLAN).

Under all these governing or administrative entities was RADECO itself. A U.S. Chief of Party representing USAID through InterAmerica and a Dominican Executive Director representing SEEBAC jointly managed the project.

PROGRAM OPERATIONS

Shortly after the project began, a field team of four InterAmerica staff members went to the Dominican Republic to establish project offices. They recruited and trained local staff members in lesson planning, script writing, studio production, community development skills, classroom observation, test design, test administration, and other skills that were needed for the production, dissemination, and evaluation of radio-assisted instruction. Three expatriate technical specialists were on-site for most of the project: the Chief of Party, a Curriculum/Scriptwriter Specialist, and a Radio Production Specialist.

InterAmerica signed a subcontract with Friend Dialogues of Shelby, North Carolina, to develop instructional design, to carry out summative evaluation, and to advise on formative evaluation and lesson development. Throughout the five years of the project, consultants specializing in mathematics education, radio education, and field research and outreach provided training, program review, evaluation, lesson development, community studies, and planning.

By late 1986, sixty people were on RADECO's staff, plus radioauxiliaries for fifty-two RADECO classrooms (twenty-eight third-grade groups, twelve fourth-grade groups, and twelve combination third- and fourth-grade groups). InterAmerica staff included the three expatriates, four full-time support staff, and fifteen part-time employees, including actors, an electrical maintenance engineer, a mechanic, two drivers, and a printer.

The RADECO Instructional System

RADECO's instructional system integrated four components to develop effective radio lessons: field research and community outreach, curriculum and lesson development, radio production, and evaluation. The following short descriptions present the basic functions of these components.

  • *Field research and outreach* identified the communities and school sites for RADECO learning centers, collected ethnographic data that aided in the design of the language curriculum, initiated community interest in the project, selected radioauxiliaries and provided training and assistance, and performed continued field observation and supervision duties for the duration of the radio lessons.

  • *Curriculum and lesson development* designed the curricula, planned lessons and lesson sequence, wrote radio scripts, and integrated field data into lesson development.

  • *Production* trained on-air teachers, taped radio lessons, maintained technical recording equipment, and integrated field data into production of lessons.

  • *Evaluation* designed the research study and collected formative and summative evaluation data from the field.

The purpose and function of each of these components are described more completely in the following chapters.

2/Community Outreach

In developing the RADECO model, it was important to assess the actual needs of the educationally unserved communities in the southwest region of the Dominican Republic. The project's community outreach effort was particularly crucial. Outreach supervisors went into the field (1) to involve the communities in making decisions concerning the project; (2) to lay the groundwork for communities to sustain the schools by selecting and training the paraprofessional aides (radioauxiliaries) and by organizing community associations to oversee the implementation; and (3) to serve as the link between the field and radio production.

STAFFING THE OUTREACH COMPONENT

When it came to selecting personnel to staff the outreach component, opposing views existed. Was it more important for a supervisor to have a background in education or in social work? Both views were credible. The major part of the work entailed the duties of a social worker—conducting surveys, collecting census data, organizing community associations. Yet, important responsibilities also

7

centered on pedagogical functions, such as training the radioauxiliaries and assisting them with classroom problems. The ideal, of course, would have been to employ educators who had experience in social work. Project administrators ultimately looked for the following qualifications: (1) knowledge of radio education; (2) human relations experience in rural communities; and (3) familiarity with applied ethnographic or quantitative data collection.

The outreach component functioned with a staff of five—a supervision and promotion coordinator and four supervisors. The supervision and promotion coordinator directed the four outreach supervisors in their work with the RADECO schools and assured that the supervisors' activities were responsive to the needs of the communities. The four supervisors organized the new schools, set up the community associations, maintained the RADECO learning centers, and assisted the radioauxiliaries.

Outreach personnel played a critical role in RADECO's success. They visited, observed, and participated in the dynamics of many different types of communities. To establish and then maintain a radio school, the supervisors often mediated conflicting goals—the goals of the project, the goals of the communities, and their own personal goals. At the same time, they had to appreciate and anticipate many demographic, economic, and political factors that could affect successful project implementation.

Identification of Radio Communities

The criteria for site selection were that the community have no school serving the school-age population, be located within a one-day round-trip from Barahona, and be reasonably accessible via roads or footpaths. In order to make informed decisions about site selection, supervisors had to go out into the field and collect exhaustive descriptive data about communities under consideration. This task proved quite arduous at times. Sources of information were extremely limited. Supervisors had no access to a library, research institute, or government sources, and the information to which they did have access was often unreliable. Communities listed as having no school did in fact have schools; others listed as having a school had none. What is more, no accurate or up-to-date maps of the region existed: villages often had different names from the ones on the map, and many communities were found not by following a map or official guidance, but by following leads from local people—school teachers, cane cutters, or mayors.

Once a prospective village was located, several factors were weighed to determine the feasibility of starting a RADECO school.

Geographic considerations. Extensive cartographic information was gathered by outreach staff. Known reference points (villages, roads, and paths) were mapped, and previously uncharted points were added. Important data included distances between sites, time references, and descriptions of road conditions. All RADECO schools had to be reasonably accessible by motorbike. However, in several cases, it was necessary to walk the last two or three kilometers in order to reach a school.

Climate was an influential factor in choosing sites because most of the learning centers were open shelters and because of the sensitivity of radio broadcasts to atmospheric conditions. There were places in the province where everything frequently stopped due to torrential rains. Transmissions could be interrupted or not heard due to storms, and roads could wash out, making contact impossible. Such sites were not appropriate for the pilot effort.

Economic considerations. The Barahona economy depends

on coffee production, sugar cane production, agriculture, and fisheries. Information was collected about the annual work cycle, daily working hours, and the extent of child involvement in the work. It was also necessary to consider any other productive activities that were undertaken by community members to augment their primary income. Children's roles in these secondary activities were of primary interest. This type of information was used to determine broadcasting schedules.

Migratory information. Information regarding migration of families from one place to another was also sought. In many instances, it was found that entire communities migrated. If a radio class was started with twenty students in a migrating community, it could be left with none after migration.

Demographic information. For each community, it was necessary to compose a description of the number of residences and inhabitants, the number of families, and the number of children. The names and ages of children were essential information in the creation of the schools, and it was sometimes the most difficult to obtain. Because a large percentage of this population was illiterate, people did not routinely document birth dates.

Sociopolitical considerations. Leaders had to be identified within each community. This was done both formally and informally. Outreach workers met with persons who held political office or who were in important social or work-related positions. At the same time they noted others who due to personality or influence were respected in the community.

Successfully identifying community leadership facilitated the gathering of other necessary information, usually led to the appointment of auxiliary and community association candidates, and provided a mechanism for disseminating information about the project. Furthermore, once contact and support for the project were established within the community leadership, individual community members were more likely to participate in and maintain the project.

Systematically delineating all the necessary information for accurate community profiles was a formidable undertaking, but communities were selected for inclusion in the project with a high degree of success. Plans for the first year of broadcasting called for twenty-three learning centers. Of these, two were combined before broadcasting started and two were closed because of low attendance, leaving twenty to operate as scheduled.

A general framework was developed to collect information from the field. During the outreach supervisor's first visit to a community, the mayor (or another person of authority) was identified and briefed as to the purpose of RADECO. After receiving permission to investigate the community as a possible site, a census was begun. On the second visit, a general meeting was held to explain the purpose and function of RADECO and to describe SEE-BAC's role in the project. Follow-up visits were made if necessary to complete the census. It was important that RADECO verified the number of students and ensured that communities understood and accepted the necessary conditions for a school.

Communities were brought into the RADECO project in two phases. Twenty communities were selected during Phase I (1983), and twenty-five were selected during Phase II (1984). (See Table 1 for a sampling of the characteristics of the communities included in the RADECO project.) Before radio transmissions could begin in selected communities, three activities had to be carried out: (1) an association of parents and friends had to be formed; (2) a shelter had to be constructed; and (3) radioauxiliaries had to be selected and trained.

TABLE 1

CHARACTERISTICS OF RADECO COMMUNITIES

Name of Community	Distance from Barahona	Approx Population	Classification	Principal Product	Secondary Product	Economic Situation
Batey Paja	35 kms	2,500	Urban/Easy access	Bananas	Tomatoes, Others	Small landholders
Preparo	46 kms	500	Rural/Easy access	Coal	Agriculture	Day laborers
Griteria	55 kms	120	Rural/Easy access	Coal	Agriculture	Day laborers
Los Cocos	51 kms	2,000	Rural/Easy access	Fishing	Agriculture, small fruits	Day laborers
Los Pistones	43 kms	120	Rural/Difficult access	Coffee	Agriculture, small fruits	Day laborers

PARENTS AND FRIENDS ASSOCIATIONS

Originally, we planned to rely on community associations or clubs to initiate and maintain the RADECO learning centers. The associations were to be guided by a local board of directors under the tutelage of the supervisors. In reality, some RADECO centers had no associations or clubs. It proved easier to form clubs in the urban centers, where people were more familiar with the concept. Association members generally numbered about ten—three or four officers and six or seven members.

The associations had four basic responsibilities: to construct the shelter; to nominate the radioauxiliary; to maintain the shelter; and to assist the radioauxiliary. One of the stipulations for initiating a RADECO school was that the community build a shelter where the children could gather for radio classes. Association members recruited volunteers to construct the shelter, gathered commitments for the donation of building materials, and most importantly, saw to it that the shelter was built before broadcasting began.

During RADECO's planning phase, building a shelter was seen as the measure of a community's commitment to participating in the RADECO project. It turned out that this was not necessarily the case. In communities where a structure already existed, building a RADECO center would have been an unjustifiable expense. In areas where no structure existed, costs varied. Construction costs were the lowest, of course, in those where the materials were readily available, in nearby fields, for instance. In other areas, residents had to buy the building materials. And in others, plantation owners, not residents, erected the building. Centers in suburban areas were the most expensive to build because all materials had to be purchased.

During the time that shelters were being constructed, the associations played an integral role in the nomination and selection of the radioauxiliary. For the most part, politics and favoritism did not govern selection. The final decision always remained with the RADECO supervisors. After the shelter had been built and the auxiliary chosen, the responsibilities of the associations centered around maintenance. They made sure that the shelters remained in good physical condition and took care of the classroom materials supplied by RADECO—clipboards, work sheets, a blackboard, a radio receiver, and batteries. Members sometimes helped the radioauxiliaries perform their duties.

RADIOAUXILIARIES

The radioauxiliaries were paraprofessionals who saw to it that students received the radio broadcasts under the best conditions possible. They arrived at least fifteen minutes before the broadcasts to organize the classroom. The auxiliaries made sure that benches and chairs were in front of the blackboard and that there was enough room between rows so that they could circulate around the class to provide help as necessary. After the children were seated, the radioauxiliaries passed out the daily worksheets and turned on the radio.

During the transmission of the lesson, students looked to the auxiliaries for help in following the lesson. Auxiliaries used gestures to signal "listen," "silence," "write," or "repeat." The auxiliaries also circulated among the students to help those having difficulty keeping up with the lessons or to correct discipline problems. After the broadcast, they took attendance and checked the students' work sheets to identify those who had problems completing the work. Most students were then dismissed. Those who had arrived late and had missed exercises or those who had questions or problems remained in the classroom. The auxiliary helped these students by conducting post-broadcast activities.

Although their duties were not overly demanding, finding radioauxiliaries was not easy. Often there was only one person in a community with adequate skills. Requirements included basic literacy skills and an interest in children and teaching. Most had about six years of schooling but demonstrated no more than a third- or fourth-grade competence in reading and mathematics. In some communities, a mayor or landowner backed the selection of a favorite son, nephew, or friend. Potential problems were usually resolved by enforcing RADECO's criteria of residence in the community and satisfactory results on a test.

Most radioauxiliaries were single, under the age of thirty, and male. The original project design called for volunteers. But voluntarism is not a universal concept and did not take root easily in a society with a developing economy and high unemployment rates. After a short labor dispute, RADECO auxiliaries were paid a small stipend by the project.

The auxiliaries functioned as aides to the radio instruction. They were provided with notes for each broadcast to familiarize them with the topic, the sequence of what was being taught, what work sheets were needed, and what information needed to be written on the blackboard prior to the broadcast. They were also given suggestions for post-broadcast activities.

Auxiliaries were not expected to fulfill the functions of a teacher, so they were not given extensive training. Their preparation consisted mainly of learning how to operate the radio, how to organize their classes, how to use their daily notes, and how to give basic help to children who were experiencing difficulty with the lessons. Initially, all auxiliaries were brought to Barahona for a two and one-half day workshop; later, small groups were trained further in the field.

FIELD SUPERVISION

Supervisors visited schools on a systematic basis to observe class sessions, advise auxiliaries, and to check student attendance. In some communities, absenteeism was a consequence of economics. During harvest time students stayed out of school to help in the fields. In most cases, however, absenteeism was correctable. To combat the problem, auxiliaries were trained to take roll regularly, to reward students for good attendance, and to emphasize to parents the merits of regular school attendance. In September 1983, RADECO began to provide an extra incentive to promote attendance. Two prizes were announced; one for the school with the best monthly attendance and another for the school with the best academic achievement.

Field visits often were made in response to a problem—an auxiliary who was not assisting the students, a shelter that was never built, or a community that was neglecting its school. In general, however, supervisors made field visits to motivate the learners, to reinforce the Parents and Friends Associations' commitment to the project, and to assist auxiliaries with providing post-broadcast activities.

3/Curriculum and Lesson Development

Curriculum development for the RADECO project was more an interpretive than a creative process. Following the standard Dominican curricula, the RADECO curriculum was molded to the needs, interests, and problems of the target audience. In all, the RADECO project generated an hour of instruction for four grade levels a day, or 680 hour-long lessons. Up to thirty minutes of each hour were spent on mathematics; the remaining half-hour was devoted mostly to reading and writing, with five to ten minutes daily of social studies, natural science, and civics.

The first step in curriculum planning for the RADECO project was an analysis of the standard Dominican curricula in the areas of language, mathematics, social studies, and the natural sciences, resulting in general objectives that could be achieved through radio education. With these objectives in mind, a "master plan" was specified that prescribed the content of the radio lessons. In addition to following the Dominican curriculum, the master plan used for mathematics lessons drew heavily on exercises from the earlier Nicaragua Radio Mathematics project. The content was that of a "typical" mathematics program, covering basic mathematics concepts, numeration, addition, subtraction, measurement, and applications.

The master plan for language lessons was solely RADECO-developed. A subcontractor, Friend Dialogues, Inc., undertook linguistic research of the Spanish spoken in the Dominican Republic and analyzed texts used in its public schools to identify the necessary content. Three areas were covered: reading, writing, and language development. The focus of the reading area was on the development of decoding and word-attack skills. The writing area developed spelling skills, with little emphasis on creative writing. Oral language development included the introduction of new vocabulary, the development of listening skills, some work with grammar, and some practice in pronunciation.

Science and social studies were written into reading lessons. Songs, stories, poems, and physical exercises also were integrated into all lessons to provide diversion during the regular radio instruction. To develop effective lessons in such a complex teaching situation, a well-trained and knowledgeable curriculum staff was vital.

The Curriculum Department

A team of seven scriptwriters developed the radio lessons. Three concentrated on mathematics, four on language. The team shared responsibility for writing the social science, science, and recreation segments. A technical coordinator reviewed all lessons to make sure that the diverse segments fit together and that the lesson flowed smoothly. Opening remarks and transitional segments that took the students from the language lessons to the recreation segments and on to mathematics were added by the coordinator.

LESSON PLANNING AND SEQUENCING

In RADECO great care was taken in planning every detail of the broadcast. Feedback from the field was integrated into lessons, time limits were imposed by the production department, and evaluative data were used to determine when a topic was considered "learned."

Lesson planning began with the development of lesson outlines based on the master plan, which designated the sequence in which topics were to be taught. Topic sequence was crafted so students learned the necessary skills in a logical and orderly fashion, mastering each level before progressing to more advanced topics. In reading, for example, the final objective of first-grade was to teach the students to read and comprehend simple sentences of the kind they might use in everyday life. The first-grade reading curriculum was divided into five topics or strands: letters, syllables, words, phrases, and sentences. However, these strands were not taught in sequential order. Instruction in letters continued only until a sufficient number of letters had been mastered so that meaningful instruction in syllables could be started. Syllables and words were introduced almost simultaneously. After a sufficient number had been taught, instruction in reading phrases was started. Somewhat later, simple sentences were introduced, and at that time, instruction in all four major strands was intermixed.

Curriculum was assembled in three stages. First, instructional material for each strand was organized into groups of related objectives, forming subtopics. For each of the subtopics, a list was made of the appropriate items of instructional content. Second, lessons comprising the academic year were grouped into blocks, and subtopics were assigned to each block. Third, exercises were constructed for each item of content. In doing this, the curriculum developer had to keep in mind the relationships between different topics and different strands and juggle assignments so that necessary prerequisites were satisfied for each lesson.

An example of the planning process for a mathematics lesson follows. The objectives for the numeration strand were identified from the master plan, then aggregated into eleven subtopics: counting by rote, reading and writing numerals, successors, counting, greater and less, completing sequences, predecessors, place value, fractions, ordinals, and number words. Each of these subtopics was then allotted a position in a block of lessons (see Table 2). Teaching material was then further broken down into specific exercises. Lesson segments consisted of these exercises. A distinctive style of lesson was then used to write these segments. Characterized by very active student involvement in radio lessons, the style is known as "interactive radio."

INTERACTIVE RADIO

Interactive radio, which takes its name from its most salient feature, involves (1) intense interaction between learners and the radio broadcast, (2) immediate correction and reinforcement of responses, (3) a segmented program format, and (4) a feed-forward formative evaluation system.

Interaction. A typical half-hour RADECO broadcast contained one hundred or more pauses for learner response. This sequence of pauses resulted in an unusual broadcast cadence on first encounter. But these pauses were the mechanism for allowing the learner to be constantly alive—answering and asking questions, engaging in structured

TABLE 2

ASSIGNMENT OF MATHEMATICS SUBTOPICS TO BLOCKS*

	Lesson Content	
Subtopic	Blocks 1 to 15	Blocks 76 to 90
Rote Counting	1-15	by 2's
Reading and writing numerals	read 1-7 write 1-5	50-100
Successors	1-8, oral	1-48, written
Counting	1-7, oral 1-4, multiple choice	1-50, written by 10's written grouping in 10's
Greater and less		0-49
Completing sequences		by 1's to 50 by 10's to 100
Predecessors		2-9
Place value		10, 20, ..., 90
Fractions		2/3, 3/4, 2/4
Ordinals		
Number Words		

*from Barbara Searle, Jamesine Friend, and Patrick Suppes, *The Radio Mathematics Project: Nicaragua, 1974–1975.*

conversations, reading, writing, calculating, solving problems, standing up, moving about purposefully, or participating in active songs, games, and exercises. This is in sharp contrast to most instructional television or radio programs that are designed for passive audiences. In interactive broadcasts, hearing the lessons without the learner responses filling in the pauses is literally hearing only half the lesson—the radio, but not the interaction.

Immediate correction and reinforcement. Students listening to the radio lessons were expected to participate actively, responding aloud to oral questions, circling pictures printed on their work sheets, underlining words, writing words or sentences in their notebooks, solving arithmetic exercises copied from dictation, and counting seeds or sticks. Student responses were frequent—one every twenty or thirty seconds. After every response, the correct answer was announced so that the students could immediately compare their own response with the correct one.

The typical pattern of the interchange consisted of presentation, response cue, response pause, reinforcement cue, and reinforcement pause. For example:

> *First radio voice:*　Children, the number *five* is greater than the number *three*. (presentation)
>
> *Second radio voice:*　Children, write the number *three*. (response cue)
>
> —pause—
>
> *First radio voice:*　Now write the number *five*.
>
> —pause—
>
> *Second radio voice:*　Which number is greater?
>
> —pause—
>
> *First radio voice:*　Five.
>
> *Second radio voice:*　Children, which number is greater? (response cue)
>
> —pause—(response pause)
>
> *First radio voice:*　That's right! Five! (reinforcement pause)
>
> —pause—(reinforcement pause)

A guided discovery method is used. This method may at first seem to comprise drill-and-practice exercises with no explanations. In reality, though, the lessons consist of carefully planned sequences of examples, designed to lead students to form their own generalizations from the principles involved. Even though the exercises follow a standard format, the students do not become bored partly because of their active involvement and partly because of frequent changes in topic. These frequent changes in topic give the broadcast a "magazine" or segmented structure.

Segmented format. A half-hour radio lesson consists of a dozen or more distinct instructional segments, each no more than a few minutes in length. In interactive radio, an objective that requires a total of thirty minutes of instructional time would normally be divided into ten or fifteen segments. These segments are then presented in the same number of lessons over the course of several weeks.

Segmentation is a standard device in children's programming of any kind. In the *Sesame Street* programs, segmentation has been used for years as a means of holding the children's attention. A segmented structure aids retention, especially in the teaching of skill subjects such as arithmetic and reading. With interactive radio, segmentation also helps to preserve continuity of instruction. Occasionally missed transmissions and patterns of learner absences are not as likely to present a problem. The distribution of instruction across segments makes it unlikely that learners will miss enough of any sequence to lose the sense of the instruction altogether.

In RADECO the segmented format facilitated team script development. Any member of the scriptwriting team could be assigned a segment or two of a given script to write. These semi-autonomous, semi-interchangeable segments were then pieced together by the technical coordinators into a coherent radio script. Segmentation also made it easier to incorporate feed-forward data into an entire lesson.

Feed-forward data. With a feed-forward design, lesson effects are observed in the field and noticeable deficiencies are immediately corrected. Data are gathered through classroom observations and periodic testing, providing a basis for deciding either to continue teaching a topic or to consider the topic learned. In addition to systematically gathered data, information gathered informally from community participants—radioauxiliaries, parents, and students—is used.

In RADECO, the feed-forward design was set up so that instructional design modifications appeared in programming not long after the discovery of the instructional problem.

Writing Lesson Segments

The outline of each lesson indicated number of segments, topics, timing, objectives, and suggestions for activities or techniques. This outline was developed by the technical coordinator from the master plan. Once a particular outline was completed, it was distributed to a writer for script development. Each RADECO radio script consisted of twelve to fifteen instructional segments or units of instruction and activity—each ranging from a few seconds to five minutes in length. A typical RADECO instructional segment was about two and one-half minutes long.

Each segment was a part of a sequence of segments distributed across various lessons, and its place in the sequence influenced the presentation of exercises. The example below illustrates the design of segments for teaching a third-grade reading passage. The passage was broken into 5-minute segments to be spread across six lessons.

SEGMENT DESIGN

Segment 1. Learners read the passage silently while the radio voices read it aloud and then ask a couple of straightforward information questions.

Segment 2. Learners read each sentence aloud in chorus several times, with reinforcement.

Segment 3. Learners are instructed to read portions of the text silently and are asked for straightforward information embedded in what they've just read.

Segment 4. After a rapid reading of the entire text, learners are asked to search back through the text for information.

Segment 5. Learners read portions of the text silently, and then are asked to draw simple inferences from what they've just read.

Segment 6. Finally, a week or so after the last presentation of the passage, learners return to it for a rapid review.

The following script is a translation from Spanish of a RADECO lesson written to conform to Segment 1 above.

Sonia: Look at lines one, two, three.

—pause—

Miguel: Read with me, you silently and me out loud.

Miguel: Start reading.
"Lola was with her little brother. She was reading him a story. 'Listen, well, don't interrupt me,' she told him."

Sonia: Children, who was Lola with?

—pause—

Miguel: With her little brother.

Miguel: She was reading something to her little brother, what was it?

—pause—

Sonia: A story.

Instructional segments were written with an introduction, a body, and a conclusion. The introduction could consist of preparatory materials, sometimes dramatized. Whether or not the segment began with preparatory materials, study and practice was always introduced by a series of locator or orientation cues—instructions to learners on how to find the right place on the worksheet and what to do when they found it. The cues were pared away bit by bit over the course of the exercise. The objective was to present as brief a cue as possible while maintaining the clarity of the instruction. "Children, look at the next picture . . . and the next . . . the next." "Children, write that word in cursive under the picture . . . write the correct word under the next picture . . . and under the next." Common practice was to end the segment with a synopsis of the task, "Now children, you've written four new words in cursive!"

Allowing sufficient time for student responses was crucial. Badly timed responses caused confusion and interrupted lesson progression. This problem was easily identified by means of the feed-forward evaluation and was usually corrected in subsequent lessons. Poor timing often resulted in an "echoing" problem. That is, responses were given immediately by only two or three children, whose answers were simply repeated by the rest of the

class. Echoing indicated that only a few children were following the instruction at the rate at which it was being
presented.

Sometimes the cause of echoing was that the exercise
was too difficult—meaning either that the exercise was
misplaced in the sequence of instruction or that the initial
teaching of the concept was inadequate. Another common
cause was that the children needed more time to formulate
the answer than was allowed. In mathematics, for example,
some exercises required mental calculations. Time to do
them had to be allowed for in the overall response time.
The same kind of problem existed in reading exercises.
When asked to read a four- or five-letter word, a first-
grader had to be given time to inspect the letters and mentally assimilate them before processing the word.

One solution used in RADECO lessons was deferred
responses, in which the children were asked first to think
silently about the answer, then after a short pause, to
answer in chorus. A sample instruction might take the
following form:

Radio voice: Look at the word in the next square. Look at
the word carefully but don't say anything. Just
think quietly about how to say the word.

—pause—

Radio voice: Now tell me: What word is it?

—pause—

Another solution was to direct the students' attention
to each letter in turn, preparatory to reading the word.
This gave the students sufficient time to process the word
mentally before saying it aloud. The script was then written
as follows:

Radio voice: Look at the word that is written there. Later you're going to read this word aloud, but first you're going to look at the letters. Look at the first letter in the word and tell me: what is it?

—pause—

Radio voice: A *p*. And the second letter?

—pause—

Radio voice: An *a*. And the next letter?

—pause—

Radio voice: An *n*. Now look at the whole word, all of the letters together. Tell me, what is that word?

—pause—

Radio voice: *Pan*. That's right. It's the word "pan."

For multisyllabic words, it was better to direct students' attention to the syllables that formed the word, having them tell where the syllable divisions were, and how to pronounce each syllable. Finally, they were asked to pronounce the entire word.

All RADECO scripts included at least two short enhancement segments in the course of each half-hour lesson. These were songs, games, or guided movement activities. A half-hour RADECO lesson was more intensive than a half-hour of conventional instruction, so the need arose for an enhancement activity every ten minutes or so of air time. Enhancement material also contained instructional content. Songs, for example, were often repetition drills set to music. A wide variety of instruction was accomplished through movement games and exercises, such as identifying body parts or reciting cadences of letters and numbers.

SCRIPT CONTINUITY

Script continuity was the process that turned all the segments, the bits and pieces, into an effective instructional broadcast. Continuity was achieved in three major ways: (1) the use of stock music and sound effects; (2) a continuing cast of characters; and (3) the controlled use of narrative drama and setting.

Stock music and sound effects. Sound effects and bits of music were used as continuity and cueing devices. Dramatic material in the RADECO broadcasts was generally signalled with the use of a stock theme, such as guitar music that was brought up for two or three seconds and then cross-faded under the voices as the dialogue began. Learners quickly knew the dramatic theme and were cued for what to expect next in the lesson. Similarly, classroom behaviors were often cued by music or sound effects. For example, learners were cued to turn over their worksheets by a little flute melody.

Continuing cast of characters. In RADECO broadcasts, each school year and each of the two main subject areas had its own continuing cast of four main characters: a male and female adult "teacher" voice, a target-age child, and an *abuelo*—a dignified grandfather figure who served as the source of practical advice and rural wisdom. The two "teacher" voices generally addressed the learners directly. Occasionally they engaged in dialogues and vignettes with each other and with other characters. For example:

(sound of water lapping at the edges of a lake)

Carlitos: Sonia, what's that sound? Is it the ocean?

Sonia: No, Carlitos . . . it's the sound of a lake.

Carlitos: A lake?!

> *Miguel:*   Yes, Carlitos, it's a lake.
>
> (sound disappears)
>
> *Sonia:*   Children, we are going to visit some of the most beautiful lakes and rivers in our country.
>
> *Miguel:*   But first, let's continue with the page of exercises.

Such dialogues and vignettes were very short, between ten and thirty seconds. Their purpose was to establish continuity or introduce new material.

Narrative, drama, and setting. Narrative and drama were used in RADECO scripts to sustain learner interest and to provide continuity between lessons. A firm working rule was to keep this material as lean and spare as possible, not to turn simple transitions into full-scale dramas. Long passages of narrative or dialogue would counter the goal of keeping the learners as active and involved as possible. In longer RADECO passages, such as those during social studies or natural science lessons, learners were incorporated into the drama by means of response cues, in effect becoming participants in the drama themselves.

> *Sonia:*   Here are Carlitos and his sister helping the *abuelo* in his garden.
>
> *Miguel:*   While they're working, the *abuelo* is saying:
>
> *Abuelo:*   Yes, the soil is important to us because the plants that nourish us grow in it.
>
> *Sonia:*   Children, where do the plants grow?
>
> —pause—
>
> *Miguel:*   In the soil.
>
> (guitar music)

Abuelo: The soil gives the plants the nourishment they need to grow.

Sonia: Children, where do the plants get the nourishment they need?

—pause—

Miguel: From the soil.

Carlitos: Ah! Now, I understand. The soil nourishes the plants, and the plants nourish us.

Abuelo: That's right, Carlitos.

Normally, the dramatic setting is the learner's own classroom or place of assembly. But often the listeners are asked to imagine an appropriate site. A common setting for RADECO science lessons was the abuelo's garden. A quick line—"Let's see what grandfather is doing in his garden"— with an accompanying musical cue was all that was needed to transform the setting.

Nonbroadcast Activities

RADECO lessons had to be written so that concepts were explained, principles illustrated, and students guided in the completion of exercises, all with minimal visual stimulus. To accomplish this, instruction was presented through exemplary concepts and principles using strictly controlled vocabulary, rather than through elaborate explanations. Technical vocabulary was used sparingly and only after the concepts to which it referred were well understood by the students. Work sheets were used to supplement the lessons, but these provided only practice exercises, not explanatory material.

To ensure that students fully grasped the concepts and principles being presented, the hour-long radio lesson was augmented by nonbroadcast activities carried out by the radioauxiliares. The auxiliaries, however, were not trained teachers and needed guidance from the curriculum and lesson developers to integrate these activities into the curriculum goals. Nonbroadcast activities were designed by the curriculum department to complement the radio lessons, taking into account the abilities of the radioauxiliaries, the limitations of the supplies and equipment available, and the variable amount of time that might be needed on the same activity in different centers.

The primary means of communicating with the radioauxiliaries was through written notes that clearly specified in simple language how to carry out and manage the necessary activities. These notes alleviated many of the initial problems observed in the classrooms.

To illustrate the manner in which RADECO lessons were segmented and integrated with prebroadcast activities, this chapter ends with a sample RADECO lesson and accompanying nonbroadcast activities.

Grade: 4

Length of the Segment: 2:00 minutes

Lesson: 80

Writer: Margarita H.

Themes: Influence of the environment on the economy

Segment: 4 of 29

Sonia: Students, now we are going to talk about the importance of fertile soil.

Clarita: Fertile!

Miguel: Yes, Clarita, there are many kinds of soil in our country.

Sonia: There are soils that are very dry, and soils that are very moist.

Miguel: But there are soils that are neither very dry nor very moist.

Sonia: And these soils are very good for agriculture. They are called fertile soils.

Miguel: Knowing this is important for us . . .

Clarita: Why?

Sonia: Because some soils produce more crops than others.

Miguel: For example, valleys almost always are fertile, so they are more productive.

Clarita: And what is a valley?

Miguel: Well, let's look at picture number two.

Sonia: Look at the first drawing.

Miguel: That is a valley. . . . Valleys are flat lands between mountains.

Sonia: Tell me what the flat lands between mountains are called.

—pause—

Miguel: Valleys.

Sonia: There are dry valleys and damp valleys and very fertile valleys. . . .

Miguel: There are dry valleys . . . damp ones and what?

—pause—

Sonia: Fertile.

Miguel: In the dry valleys it is more difficult to grow crops because of the lack of water.

Clarita: In the dry valleys, crops don't grow?

Sonia: Yes, they grow, Clarita, but the farmers have to water them.

Clarita: Are all flat lands called valleys?

Sonia: No, there are also plains. . . . These are flat lands, but larger than valleys.

Miguel: Look at the other picture.

—pause—

Sonia: That is a plain.

Miguel: There are also very fertile plains.

Clarita: Look at the cows!

Miguel: Yes, because plains are good for raising cattle.

Sonia: Plains are good for raising what?

—pause—

Miguel: Cattle

Sonia: The dry valleys are good for growing cotton, cocoa. . . .

Miguel: In the southern part of the country, there are dry valleys.

Sonia: Where can you find dry valleys?

—pause—

Miguel: In the south.

Sonia: On the other hand, fertile valleys are found mostly in the northern region of our country.

Miguel: Students, another day we will return to talk about that.

4/Production

The interactive radio lessons used in the RADECO project were designed as substitutes for the regular classroom teachers. RADECO production studios became a radio classroom. In the following dialogue, two studio actors play Juan and Julia, instructors leading the students to answers.

Julia: John, can you add three numbers?

Juan: Yes, I think so. I read each number out loud, then I add and give the answer. Correct?

Julia: Correct. Let's try it. John, how much is three, two, and one?

Juan: Three, two, and one . . . six.

Julia: Six. That's correct. Children, your turn. How much is three, two, and one?

The kinds of effective instructional practices that the production component had to reproduce in the studio included (1) clearly specifying how students would know which tasks were required and whether students performed the tasks correctly and (2) obtaining and maintaining students' participation in instructional tasks by appropriately pacing instruction.

These practices were integrated into the RADECO lessons in a number of ways. For example, auditory signals, that could replace the visual signals of regular classrooms were developed to help students follow lessons. A distinctive signal was used every time students were asked to undertake a particular task, such as completing their worksheets. Another set of sound signals clearly marked lesson segments—the end of the math lesson and the beginning of the language arts lesson, for instance. All radio broadcasts followed the same basic framework so that instructional tasks were similar across lesson segments. The pacing of instruction was a particularly important responsibility of the production team.

Programming Operation

The production component instituted a systematic programming operation that was structured yet flexible. The production program incorporated four phases: preproduction, production, postproduction, and feedback.

Preproduction. Preproduction included analyzing needs and resources, such as the availability of local talent, adequate studio facilities, and trained technicians. It also entailed reviewing the script, deciding on use of sound effects and music, and rehearsing scripts.

Production. Production of one RADECO lesson took about four hours and involved the producer, sound technician, actors, musician, and maintenance engineer. The exact timeframe depended upon the success of preproduction activities and the expertise of actors and technicians.

Postproduction. After the lesson had been recorded and edited, a staff member listened to it with script and worksheet in hand to check for errors. Any errors were taken care of by further editing.

Feedback. Sample classroom observations and periodic testing provided data that were used by production staff to improve radio production.

These production-related activities accounted for approximately 60 percent of production personnel time. Twenty-five percent of their time was devoted to training activities. Continuous training was an important element for actors and technical personnel. Local actors were schooled in theatrics and locution, while technical personnel were trained in the basic maintenance and use of electronic equipment. Administrative activities comprised the remaining 15 percent of the staff's responsibilities. These activities included planning for adequate use of studio equipment; selecting and contracting actors, music, and engineers; and coordinating the activities of the other components, specifically curriculum development and evaluation. In addition to the responsibilities outlined above, the production component was responsible for making sure that the taped lessons arrived at the broadcasting station on time, so that programs could be aired as scheduled.

Key production personnel in the RADECO project were: the producer, who directed all the aspects of programming; the production assistant, who was in charge of the timing of segments, planning music and sound effects, and handling the responsibilities of the director when necessary; the sound technician, who handled all electronic equipment; the actors, who performed all scripts; a musician, who composed musical segments and played all instruments; and a maintenance engineer, who repaired and installed all electronic equipment. The minimum personnel needed for a recording session were one producer, one assistant, one sound technician, four principal actors, one secondary actor, and one guitarist.

RECORDING SCHEDULE

First-grade lessons were recorded and broadcast to the first twenty learning centers in 1983. Second-grade lessons were recorded and broadcast to these centers from February through October 1984. In early 1984, a SEEBAC commission determined that programming for the entire first two grades should be revised and broadcast to an expanded number of schools. From March to October 1984, new communities were surveyed, and thirty-four new schools were organized. In November 1984, a revised first-grade program was broadcast to the thirty-four new schools and to first-grade classes organized in eleven of the original schools. In April 1985, the third-grade program was broadcast to children continuing in the original schools. From that date, the RADECO staff produced two grade levels at the same time—a double production effort. This double schedule was accommodated by having a split shift that kept the studio busy from 8 A.M. to 8 P.M. The double production schedule necessitated bringing on more staff and providing existing staff with additional training. Broadcast of the revised first-grade program ended in August 1985, and the revised second-grade program began in mid-September 1985. The third-grade program was broadcast to the original schools in 1985, and a fourth-grade program was recorded and broadcast during 1986.

BASIC ELEMENTS IN PROGRAM PRODUCTION

After a script had been corrected and approved by the curriculum department, it was sent to the radio department for technical adjustments and recording. The producer organized the production tasks: contacting actors and the musician, rehearsing and recording songs, recording sound effects, re-recording any previously broadcasted segments that needed to be revised based on feedback. To prepare to record new material, the sound technician organized the music and sound effects, and the producer rehearsed with the actors.

The assistant timed each segment during recording to compare it with the initial time of the script. The recording of each math or language arts lesson had to remain as close to thirty minutes as possible. If the recorded lesson was too long or too short or a mechanical problem surfaced during the recording, the program had to be edited. It was also at the editing stage that the half hour of math was combined with the half hour of language arts to form one radio broadcast.

TRAINING ON-AIR PERSONALITIES

Education by radio demands that the students not be distracted from the task at hand. The on-air personalities that interpreted the scripts had to be engaging enough to capture and hold the students' attention. Among the qualities RADECO personnel sought in actors were clear and precise diction, experience in radio, theater, and singing, extroverted personalities, the ability to grasp new information quickly, and knowledge of the social context of the audience to whom the program was directed.

While professional actors were used throughout most of the project, the training of amateur actors was an early expedient during the project's days in Barahona. Recruiting professional actors in Barahona, a provincial city, was difficult. The primary pool of talent consisted of amateur actors and local residents with an interest in oral communication. A series of workshops were developed to provide RADECO actors with training in oral communication. Typical problems encountered were reading mistakes, limited knowledge of grammar, unclear diction, regional dialect, poor vocabulary, improper intonation, lack of or affected expression, lack of improvisational ability, inability to concentrate, and a lack of discipline or confidence. Continuous inservice training motivated the actors to progress from their initial passivity to active participation in the lessons, from being shy to trusting, and from accepting routine to expressing themselves creatively.

Two-day workshops for the actors were composed of the following learning sequence:

- Viewing a model actor in didactic programming,
- Role playing on-air experiences, and
- Providing individual assistance.

In addition to developing workshops, radio department personnel developed instructional pamphlets to supplement available printed material in basic locution techniques. A pamphlet called "Training the Voice," for instance, presented rudimentary information, diction and intonation exercises, and oral expression practice.

Because the recording process is tied to the studio, the production staff was somewhat isolated from the rest of the project. A series of visits to radio schools gave the actors an opportunity to interact with the students and allowed the actors to evaluate their on-air performance. On-location observations resulted in the following modifications to performance:

• Stronger emphasis was placed on character interpretation when actors realized that many students could not differentiate voices;

• Greater rapport resulted as the actors developed a deeper understanding of and affection for the students;

• Better disposition to accept diction correction.

Training community residents with little or no experience in radio broadcasting was a special challenge for the RADECO project. Project personnel were rewarded by seeing local residents develop their capacity to make critical judgments and assume responsibility for their professional development.

5/Evaluation

The first year of broadcasting for the RADECO project, 1983, was highly experimental. RADECO administrators had to make numerous judgments about the methodology and quality of their project in relation to its specific objective—providing an education equivalent to the regular Dominican school system. They also had to deal with constraints in individual components of the project, such as limited recording facilities, radioauxiliaries with minimal training, and initially high levels of student attrition. The inexperience of local actors and scriptwriters has been mentioned in Chapter Four. In addition, the project experienced a high staff turnover in its initial months. In order to assess the impact of these and other factors on the effectiveness of the methodology, RADECO employed two types of evaluation—formative and summative.

Evaluation is the process of measuring progress toward achieving objectives, and evaluation planning involves determining how this process will take place. Evaluation planning plays an especially important role in innovative education activities, such as the RADECO project. Teaching techniques and methods are still being refined even during implementation, and results from ongoing observations and achievement testing serve as the basis for future activities. For this reason, both formative and summative evaluations for the RADECO project were designed as soon as goals and objectives were established.

The design for formative evaluation of the project used data derived from classroom observations and weekly tests to guide lesson development and production. The feedforward mode of information collection, patterned after that developed by the Radio Mathematics Project in Nicaragua, was designed to promote an ongoing process of change. The summative evaluation design used a standardized post-test to compare student achievement in RADECO with student achievement in the public schools. Evaluation staff carried out both types of evaluation activities.

The Evaluation Component

The Barahona field office housed the project's evaluation and outreach components. Four evaluators and a department head undertook both the formative and summative evaluations. One evaluator also served as a data analyst. Evaluators visited RADECO schools twice weekly to observe classes, to make detailed notes of student behavior, and to administer the weekly tests. This formative data was collated by the head of the evaluation component and compiled in weekly reports. Evaluative information contained in the reports was used by other components to make changes in lesson format, methodology, scripts, length of pauses, music, voices, and sound effects. Summative data collection was compiled by the same staff and forwarded to Friend Dialogues in Shelby, North Carolina, for computer analysis.

While the evaluation staff systematically collected data, outreach personnel provided supplemental information. Through their contacts with radioauxiliaries, parents, and student-outreach supervisors gathered important data that helped script writers and production staff improve scripts and radio production.

FORMATIVE EVALUATION PROCESS

The formative evaluation process used in the RADECO project differed from the usual process of revision in which a model is field-tested, analyzed, modified, and then sent back out in the field for use. Production of RADECO lessons was not interrupted for field-testing, analysis, and modification. Data gathered in the field were integrated into the ongoing production of lessons. Evaluation data served as the basis for deciding whether to continue teaching a topic, to modify a lesson, or to go on to another topic. Two kinds of data were collected to provide the necessary information about lesson effectiveness—qualitative data from field observations and quantitative data from weekly tests.

Field observations. Accurate information was an important consideration in conducting field observations. To ensure accuracy, a standardized form called for the name of the observer, date of the observation, site of the observation, number of students attending, and identification of the lesson being observed. Additional space was provided for special notes or observations.

Staff were trained to be as unobtrusive as possible in performing classroom observations. The risk of departures from students' normal performance due to the presence of a stranger in the classroom was controlled through staff scheduling. One evaluator at a time was sent to a school, and evaluators were instructed not to interfere with the progress of a lesson. In addition, visits were planned on a randomly established schedule that took into consideration (1) the number of observers available, (2) the number of sites that could be visited daily, and (3) the distance of the sites from the field office. A table of random numbers was used to make up the weekly schedule of observations, so both sites and observers were randomly sampled.

Weekly tests. Weekly tests covered topics presented in the radio lessons. Generally, testing of each topic was spread out over several weeks for each topic. For example, a topic such as reading the letter *i* was tested a week before being presented to check preknowledge and transference of previously acquired skills, a week after being introduced to check immediate learning, and two or three weeks after presentation to test retention. A test outline form was used to keep track of broadcast topics. The file of test outline forms was continuously updated using formative results.

Individual items for a specific topic were selected from a prewritten item pool. Selection-type items like those shown below in Figure 1 were used because they were objective, error-free, time efficient, and enhanced the reliability of a test. Since the children did not yet read well, instructions for each item were given orally.

Topic: Read the letter "i"
Instructions: Look at the box that has a picture of a tree. Look at the letters in this box. Find the letter *i*. Circle the letter *i*. (Pause)

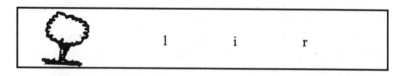

Fig. 1 Sample Weekly Test Item

Test reliability was enhanced through the use of standardized test administrations. Test instructors and items were read at a standard pace. Mean percentage scores were calculated for each topic, and mean percentages were calculated for each section. The percentages from each test site were graphed and used along with recommendations from field observations to write weekly reports.

SUMMATIVE EVALUATION

RADECO evaluated the overall quality of instruction to check the performance of children in the first experimental RADECO centers and to ascertain whether future students could also be expected to perform well with radio-assisted instruction. A research design was developed to compare the educational outcomes of students in RADECO learning centers with the educational outcomes of students in conventional schools in the same area of the country.

Three summative evaluation studies on instructional materials were conducted. First-grade materials were evaluated in 1983, second-grade materials in 1984, and third-grade in 1986. A true comparison of RADECO learners with public school students was difficult because of the number of differing conditions to which the two groups were exposed. Variability was present in each of the following areas:

Community characteristics. RADECO instruction was made available to students in small, remote communities. These communities had few social services, no income-producing industries, little communication with larger population centers, and a high rate of illiteracy. Any of these socio-economic characteristics could have affected the abilities and attitudes of incoming RADECO students. Control schools were drawn from communities similar to RADECO's populations, but factors such as having or not having a school made exact comparability impossible.

Physical characteristics of the learning environment. The buildings in which the RADECO students received instruction were quite different from the public schools. RADECO learning centers were usually wall-less, one-room shelters. Public schools, on the other hand, had multiple classrooms, toilet facilities, better instructional materials, and were generally more comfortable.

Teacher characteristics. The source of instruction in both settings was quite different. Most public school students were taught by credentialled teachers. The main source of instruction in RADECO classes was the radio; individualized instruction was provided by the radioauxiliaries, who had a limited educational background. However, the instruction that the RADECO students received was probably more systematically developed and delivered than public school instruction.

Student characteristics. The number of students in a RADECO and public school classroom varied; there were generally fewer students in the RADECO learning centers than in public schools. The RADECO students also differed from public school students as to age and gender: they were generally older and most were female.

Time spent in class. One primary difference between the two groups of students was the amount of time spent in class. RADECO students spent only one hour per day in class, while conventional school students spent four to five hours (although frequent teacher absences reduced the actual time students spent in regular schools).

Proportion of time spent on core curriculum. The range of subjects taught in the public schools was not identical to the subjects taught in the RADECO classes. The RADECO project taught only the core curriculum—mathematics, reading, language, and limited science and social studies. Public school students had instruction in art, more time dedicated to physical education, and greater opportunity for socialization.

Promotion policy. The different promotion policies of
RADECO and the public schools resulted in many of the
public school students having to repeat a grade, a rarity
in the RADECO program. This could have affected the
incoming skills level of many of the public school students
in the study.

Because the summative research design employed could
not totally control these variables, the following discussion
of the two summative evaluations includes a number of
caveats and limitations.

FIRST-GRADE EVALUATION STUDY

To evaluate the educational quality of the first-grade
lessons, a study was undertaken to compare the educational outcomes of the RADECO learning centers with the
educational outcomes of conventional schools in the same
area of the country. Data used in this study were derived
from two tests: the first, given at the beginning of the school
year, was designed to determine whether the two groups
(conventional school students and RADECO students) had
roughly comparable abilities and knowledge at the beginning of the school year. The second test, given at the end
of the school year, was intended to measure the amount
of core curriculum that had been learned during the year.

The experimental group. The program to which the experimental group was exposed during the first year of
broadcasting (1983) was not consistent. At the beginning
of the year, scripts were not well written, the planned
sequence of instruction was not always followed precisely,
and work sheets were not well designed because of the
inexperience of the production team. Consequently, procedures were changed as the year progressed, and all of
these factors improved by the end of the academic year.

In addition to scripting changes, the length of lessons was changed during the year. At the beginning, after one hour of instruction delivered all by radio, the class was over. A few months later, however, post-broadcast activities were initiated to provide time for the review of radio-taught topics. Furthermore, when non-broadcast activities were first started, each radioauxiliary was left to determine appropriate ways for the class to respond, but after several months, radioauxiliaries were given instructional guide books to standardize the activities.

The number òf subjects in the experimental group decreased during the year, as well. Of an anticipated twenty-three experimental centers, data from only nineteen were available for analysis—two centers were combined, two were closed due to attendance, and an administrative error nullified the validity of the post-test at another. There was considerable turnover of students during the year. Many of the students who were pretested dropped out, so the number of students who took the post-test was considerably smaller than the number who took the pretest. Also, because of the high rates of turnover and absenteeism, it was not unequivocally certain that the students who took the post-test formed a true subset of the ones who took the pretest.

The comparison group. Fifteeh comparison schools were selected—seven in the coffee-growing region and eight in the cane-growing region. The schools were selected from communities as similar as possible to the places where the RADECO centers were located. Many of them were small, rural schools in very poor communities.

The abilities and attitudes of incoming students differed between experimental and control schools. In the project's first year, RADECO students tended to be older than those in public schools.

That public schools tended to be in more accessible areas than RADECO learning centers also contributed to a difference in attitudes and abilities. Public school students had more access to amenities such as newspapers and health services, which could have affected the incoming skills of the students as well as their attitudes toward education. In addition, some of these communities had preschools operated by another development project, which had some effect on the skills of the incoming students.

An additional factor that had to be taken into account in selecting comparison classes was that schools in the Dominican Republic have different annual schedules, depending upon the growing season of the predominant crop in the area. Schools in the cane-growing regions start in September, whereas schools in the coffee-growing regions start in January. Since the RADECO centers were located in both areas, comparison classes were drawn from both.

Testing design. A variety of problems occurred in testing the comparison classes the first year. The following paragraphs illustrate the difficulty of data collection in a rural Third World setting. Because of logistical difficulties, only eight of the fifteen comparison classes were pretested (those in the coffee-growing region), and only three were posttested (only one of which was from the group that was pretested). Since the data obtained were too sparse to provide a good comparison, a second wave of sixteen comparison classes were chosen the following year. In general, classes were selected so that the total comparison group had two sets of first-grade children from the same schools— one group first started in the 1982–83 school year and the other in the 1983–84 school year. Due to administrative problems, none of the second wave of comparison classes was pretested. Only one of the twenty-six classes was both pretested and post-tested. All these factors made data interpretation extremely difficult.

The tests. The evaluation design called for both a pretest and a post-test. The pretest consisted of fifteen multiple-choice items. The instructions were read aloud by a test administrator while the children marked answers in test booklets. The booklets contained fifteen pages–one for each item (see sample test items in Fig. 2). Of the fifteen items, one covered reading words; two, reading numbers; three, basic mathematical concepts; and the remaining nine, comprehension of oral language.

The post-test was more complex. It followed a matrix-sampling design, that is, there were several forms distributed randomly (more or less) within each classroom. There were four worksheet forms with the items arranged in such a way that the same oral instructions would apply to items on the different forms. For example, each work sheet showed a picture of a different object (a duck, a pineapple, a candle, and a rat), but the oral instruction—"Write the name of the thing shown in the picture"—was the same for all four forms. The four forms were distributed randomly in each classroom. The purpose of using four forms was partly to allow more data to be collected and partly to alleviate the problem of children copying from one another.

Not all of the items on the test had four forms. Items that were completely determined by the oral instruction did not differ from one work sheet to another. An example of this type of item was "Write the sum of 7 plus 4." Eleven of the twenty-four items were identical on all forms. Of the twenty-four items on the post-test, six were in mathematics, one in oral language, ten in reading, and seven in writing. (See sample items, Figure 3).

The instructions for the pretest were read by a test administrator dispatched from the evaluation component. To administer all post-tests at the same time, the instructions for the post-test were given by radio. To some extent, this may have biased the test in favor of the RADECO students, who were accustomed to listening to and following instructions given by radio.

Fig. 2:   SMALL OF FIRST GRADE PRE-TEST ITEMS

ITEM 1.
Oral Instructions:

Marca la vaca.
(Circle the cow.)

ITEM 2.
Oral Instructions:

Marca lo que
puede volar.
(Circle the animal
that can fly.)

Fig. 3:   SAMPLE OF FIRST GRADE POST–TEST ITEMS

ITEM 20
Oral Instructions:

Escriba el nombre
de ese objeto.
(Write the name
for each object.)

Grading of tests. All tests were graded by computer to prevent grader bias. Since the pretest items were multiple-choice, this process was straightforward. For the post-test, however, many of the items required constructed responses, which meant there was more than one correct response for many items. Because of the greater response diversity, the computer grading program was more complex than for the pretest.

A grading system was developed for the post-test to enhance inter- and intra-rater reliability. All student responses were entered into the computer without grading. After responses for both the experimental and comparison students were entered, a list of responses was made for every item. Without knowing which responses were given by which group, one person marked all responses considered correct. Individual student responses were then graded, using the list of acceptable responses as the criteria for correctness.

Results. The first analysis made of the test data was an item-by-item comparison of the number of correct responses made by RADECO and public school students. The average proportion of correct answers made by the experimental group was 51 percent, while the comparison group averaged only 24 percent. A summary of the post-test scores by topics is shown in Table 3. The difference in mathematics scores was somewhat larger than the difference in reading scores.

There were several limitations on the results. Any differential levels in skill and knowledge between the experimental and comparison groups were to have been measured by a pretest. Unfortunately, the pretest and post-test data in the comparison schools were collected from two different groups of students.

A difference in ability at the beginning of the year could have accounted for some of the difference in post-test scores, thus reducing the 51 to 24 percent disparity. Another factor

TABLE 3

Post-test Scores by Topics
(Including Null Responses as Incorrect)

	Number of Items	Experimental	Comparison	Difference
Mathematics	6	.57	.22	.35
Language, reading and writing	18	.49	.24	.25
Total	24	.51	.24	.27

that could be considered was the possible bias in the testing procedure, in that instructions were given by radio. This was an advantage for the RADECO students. It was possible that the children in conventional schools could not follow the broadcast instructions and simply did not respond to the item either because they had lost their place on the worksheet, or they did not understand how to indicate their response. To investigate this possibility, the number of omitted responses was examined for each group.

The results showed that, on the average, 13 percent of the experimental group did not respond, whereas 49 percent of the comparison group made no response. The size of the disparity indicated a test bias and compromised further interpretation of the data. In view of the large percentage of comparison students who did not respond, it was thought a fairer comparison would be based only on data from responding students.

The results of an item-by-item comparison including and excluding null responses is shown in Table 4. Differences between the two groups were 58 percent correct for the RADECO students versus 45 percent for the comparison students. A summary by topic, excluding null responses,

TABLE 4

Item	Instructions	Including Null Responses (As Incorrect)		Excluding Null Responses	
		Exp	Comp	Exp	Comp
1.	Circle the animal that's sleeping	.81	.49	.83	.74
2.	Circle the letter X.	.85	.32	.87	.69
3.	He had five chicks and found five more. How many did he have then?	.80	.39	.84	.65
4.	Write the letter "N".	.57	.25	.64	.41
5.	Circle the word "al".	.62	.32	.72	.72
6.	Write the answer to seven plus four.	.73	.29	.82	.55
7.	Circle the word "to eat".	.60	.31	.62	.62
8.	Circle the word "beach".	.59	.31	.62	.62
9.	Write the number that comes after 59.	.57	.22	.64	.47
10.	Write the word "egg".	.56	.37	.61	.65
11.	Circle the word that names the animal in the picture. frog rooster cow dog	.65	.16	.72	.40
12.	Write the number that comes before 40.	.41	.09	.49	.21

TABLE 4 *(Continued)*

Item	Instructions	Including Null Responses (As Incorrect)		Excluding Null Responses	
		Exp	Comp	Exp	Comp
13.	Circle the animal that goes with the word. cat horse mule mule	.57	.25	.63	.53
14.	Write the word "see".	.22	.13	.24	.24
15.	Write 54 minus one.	.56	.15	.67	.29
16.	Write the word "fire".	.14	.11	.18	.23
17.	Write the word "the".	.43	.25	.55	.49
18.	Five minus my favorite number is two. Write my favorite number.	.36	.17	.45	.30
19.	Write the name of this thing. duck pineapple candle rat	.34	.06	.43	.22
20.	Write the name of this thing. flower tree hand pencil	.38	.08	.46	.17
21.	Circle "with a nail".	.35	.28	.44	.53
22.	Circle "the fat man".	.54	.36	.63	.59
23.	Circle the picture that goes with the phrase. broken glass big dog dirty shirt sleeping man	.48	.26	.57	.44
24.	Write "a large mule".	.13	.07	.16	.10
	MEANS:	.51	.24	.58	.45

TABLE 5

POST-TEST SCORES BY TOPICS

(Excluding Null Responses As Incorrect)

	Number Of Items	Experimental	Comparison	Difference
Mathematics	6	.65	.41	.24
Language, reading and writing	18	.55	.47	.08
TOTAL	24	.58	.45	.13

is shown in Table 5. The difference in performance in mathematics was still sizeable, but the differences in reading-related topics remained small (possibly due to age and pretest variables). The difference in mathematics scores was substantial and unlikely to be completely accounted for by age and incoming ability. A questionable aspect of making comparisons based on non-null responses was that students who did not respond might have been the least able students. RADECO students would then be compared with higher-ability comparison students.

SECOND-GRADE EVALUATION STUDY

The second-grade evaluation study was limited by the same factors as the evaluation of the first-grade lessons. Elements germane to the study will be discussed to provide insight into the research design and data analysis. The experimental group in the second-grade evaluation included all students in all RADECO learning centers. The comparison group consisted of students in fourteen classrooms in public schools located in communities similar to those in which the RADECO centers were established.

The performance of the children in the two groups was compared by giving a post-test at the end of the academic year—a post-test design for a nonequivalent group. The test, especially designed for this purpose, was composed of items that tested the goals established for second-grade by the Dominican Secretariat of Education.

The test. The test contained forty-four items—fourteen in mathematics, sixteen in reading and language, and fourteen in writing. Since the children did not yet read well, the instructions for each item were given orally. After each instruction, the children were allowed time to give their responses before the class moved on to the next item. Thus, the test was timed item-by-item rather than overall. Because of the number of children to be tested and the lack of staff, oral instructions were given by radio. In each classroom at the time of the test, a project monitor distributed test papers and supervised the students. As with the first-grade evaluation, this method of test administration, though standardized, was somewhat biased in favor of the experimental group.

The test used a matrix-sampling design similar to the first-grade study. Several forms were randomly distributed within each classroom. The items were designed so that all forms required the same oral instruction, so regardless of the form of the printed test, the instructions given by radio were appropriate.

Results. Table 6 compares the performance measures of both groups for each test item. As shown, the experimental group performed better on the post-test than the comparison group. On the average, the experimental students gave 10 percent more correct answers than the comparison students. One notable result was that the comparison group excelled in the items that tested writing skills. The experimental group excelled on the simpler words (e.g., *comer,*

TABLE 6

ITEM-BY-ITEM COMPARISON
SECOND-GRADE POST-TESTS

Item	Instructions	Topic*	RADECO Students	Comparison Students	Difference
1.	Circle the animal that's sleeping	R	.81	.71	.10
2.	Circle the letter X.	R	.82	.54	.28
3.	He had five chicks and found five more. How many did he have then?	M	.84	.59	.25
4.	Write the letter "N".	W	.70	.56	.14
5.	Circle the word "al".	R	.78	.73	.05
6.	Write the answer to seven plus four.	M	.73	.61	.12
7.	Circle the word "to eat".	R	.73	.70	.03
8.	Circle the word "beach".	R	.77	.73	.04
9.	Write the number that comes after 59.	M	.67	.63	.04
10.	Write the word "egg".	W	.72	.65	.07
11.	Circle the word that names the animal in the picture. frog rooster cow dog	R	.71	.49	.22
12.	Write the number that comes before 40.	M	.53	.34	.19

*Note: R = Reading, W = Writing, M = Mathematics

TABLE 6 *(Continued)*

Item	Instructions	Topic*	RADECO Students	Comparison Students	Difference
13.	Circle the animal that goes with the word. cat horse mule mule	R	.77	.50	.27
14.	Write the word "see".	W	.36	.29	.07
15.	Write 54 minus one.	M	.64	.50	.14
16.	Write the word "fire".	W	.37	.42	−.05
17.	Write the word "the".	W	.68	.64	.04
18.	Five minus my favorite number is two. Write my favorite number.	M	.47	.53	−.06
19.	Write the name of this thing. duck pineapple candle rat	W	.40	.23	.17
20.	Write the name of this thing. flower tree hand pencil	W	.41	.28	.13
21.	Circle "with a nail".	R	.69	.60	.09
22.	Circle "the fat man".	R	.72	.67	.05
23.	Circle the picture that goes with the phrase. broken glass big dog dirty shirt sleeping man	R	.73	.50	.23

*Note: R = Reading, W = Writing, M = Mathematics

TABLE 6 *(Continued)*

Item	Instructions	Topic*	RADECO Students	Comparison Students	Difference
24.	Write "a large mule".	W	.17	.31	−.14
25.	Circle the bird.	R	.75	.64	.11
26.	Circle the word "Shirt".	R	.75	.70	.05
27.	Write the answer to 800 plus 25.	M	.46	.22	.24
28.	Circle the word "sunrise".	R	.65	.54	.11
29.	Circle the word "he comes".	R	.73	.67	.06
30.	Solve the problem. $\begin{array}{r} 842 \\ +\ 41 \\ \hline \end{array}$	M	.65	.33	.32
31.	Circle the sentence "They go to the market".	R	.60	.37	.23
32.	Solve the problem. $\begin{array}{r} 504 \\ +132 \\ \hline \end{array}$	M	.67	.46	.21
33.	Circle the sentence "The woman sells fruit".	R	.77	.76	.01
34.	Solve the problem. $\begin{array}{r} 26 \\ +\ 3 \\ \hline \end{array}$	M	.64	.43	.21
35.	Write the word "Maco".	W	.61	.68	−.07
36.	Solve the problem. $\begin{array}{r} 723 \\ -621 \\ \hline \end{array}$	M	.47	.33	.14
37.	Write the word "country".	W	.23	.48	−.25

*Note: R = Reading, W = Writing, M = Mathematics

TABLE 6 *(Continued)*

Item	Instructions	Topic*	RADECO Students	Comparison Students	Difference
38.	Solve the problem. 376 − 56	M	.52	.30	.22
39.	Write the word "grandson"	W	.51	.60	−.09
40.	Solve the problem. 32 × 3	M	.48	.34	.14
41.	Write the word "Jumps".	W	.19	.36	−.17
42.	Solve the problem. 67 − 8	M	.31	.09	.22
43.	Write the sentence. "The cat is in the box."	W	.00	.00	.00
44.	Write the sentence. "The sun gives light."	W	.13	.15	−.02
	MEANS:		.58	.48	.10

*Note: R = Reading, W = Writing, M = Mathematics
Note: Difference = experimental − control

ver, el), whereas the comparison group did better on the more difficult words and phrases (e.g., *fuego, un mulo, grande, pais, nieto*). This might have been a reflection of different instructional emphasis. In the radio lessons, stress was placed on reading rather than on writing for most of the first two years of instruction. Only late in second-grade and in third-grade were the children asked to write.

TABLE 7

PROPORTIONS CORRECT BY TOPIC
SECOND GRADE POST-TESTS

	Number Of Items	RADECO Students	Comparison Students	Difference
Mathematics	14	.58	.41	.17
Reading & Language	16	.74	.62	.12
Writing	14	.39	.40	− .01
TOTAL	44	.58	.48	.10

Because of the differences between the two groups in different subjects, averages for the three main topics were calculated separately. These data, shown in Table 7, demonstrated that the experimental group performed considerably better in mathematics than the comparison group. In language and reading the experimental group did somewhat better, while in writing little difference was noted.

CONCLUSIONS

In the first-grade evaluation, mention was made of the question of test bias—the form of the instructions being more familiar to the experimental group. These children were more experienced in following the instructions and less likely to lose their place on the page, and the pace of the instructions was more appropriate for the experimental group than for the comparison group. The phrasing, speed of speech, and the amount of time allowed for making a response followed the standards used in the radio lessons.

The major indication of bias in the first-grade evaluation was the number of children in the comparison group who omitted responses to some of the test items, with a tendency for this number to increase as the test progressed. The evaluators surmised that some of the children lost their place on the test paper and could not catch up again. There was much less evidence of this tendency in the second-grade evaluation. On the average second-grade test item, 27 percent of the comparison group did not answer as compared to 15 percent of the experimental group.

Evidence of bias was found in the data on items 11, 13, 19, 20, and 23 (see Table 4). These five items contained the most complex instructions used in the test. It was clear that the experimental group's performance exceeded the comparison group's (60 percent versus 40 percent correct). This indicated a problem with the construct validity of the post-test. The form of the test and the test items seemed to account for some of the difference in performance. Evaluators mitigated the bias effect by analyzing data with null responses excluded. When this was done, the disparities in results were reduced. While mathematics did not change, there was much less of a difference in reading and language, and writing scores.

Taking all evidence into consideration, RADECO students seemed to do as well as conventional school students in the areas of reading, language, and writing, and they did significantly better in mathematics. Since subjects such as science and social studies were not evaluated, conclusions could not be drawn in these areas. With these limitations on the results in mind, the performance of the RADECO students was impressive, especially when one takes into consideration that the RADECO students were in class for less than half of the time that the comparison students were, and that RADECO study time was at the end of the day when the children were likely to be tired from their day's work in the fields.

6/Institutionalization

Institutionalization can mean (1) the adoption of project methods and materials, or (2) the integration of a project's offices, staff, and resources into local structures through the establishment of the project as a permanent entity. In the case of RADECO, it appears that both have occurred.

In March 1986, the RADECO project was formally established as the Radio Education Program (*Programa Radioeducativo*). RADECO personnel, already thoroughly trained in the development and production of instructional radio materials, are staffing the new department and the project sound studio. RADECO's equipment has been taken over by the Radio Education Program.

The project's materials and methods, including both its application of the interactive radio methodology and its community development system, have also been preserved by institutionalization. Under the terms for the establishment of the Radio Education program, the Barahona field office operation has been kept open and transmission of the original RADECO radio lessons to communities in the southwest region has been continued.

The intent of this chapter is to consider how institutionalization of RADECO came about and to draw insights from the RADECO for future projects.

The Process of Institutionalization

Although nothing in the project's original agreements committed the government of the Dominican Republic (GDR) to institutionalization, the idea was implicit, as illustrated by the project requirement that SEEBAC staff be trained to assume responsibility "for designing and disseminating additional radio education programs" (see chapter one).

Prior to signing the RADECO project agreement, the GDR carried out a needs assessment in the southwest region; the findings confirmed that RADECO's objective of providing basic education by radio to communities where there were no schools would respond to the educational needs of the southwest region. The needs assessment document also implied that institutionalization would be a desirable outcome of a successful project.

The strategy for achieving eventual institutionalization of the project entailed involving the top level decision-makers at SEEBAC in the project and obtaining professionally qualified staff directly from SEEBAC. Moving the production department from Barahona to Santo Domingo in 1984 increased contact with high-level SEEBAC decision-makers and made it possible for SEEBAC technicians to work on the project.

An economic study carried out in 1985 calculated that costs for expanding the RADECO project to cover virtually all unschooled areas of the country would be manageable. The model's economy of scale increases notably as the number of involved communities grows. The per pupil (unit) cost of making four grades of radio primary education available to the nearly half million unenrolled school-age children would be about half the current unit cost in the formal system. While projections of this sort are based on many assumptions and at best can indicate only general trends and magnitudes, the figures were reassuring enough to support SEEBAC's subsequent decision to incorporate RADECO into its regular program.

The central factor in the question of institutionalization has always been SEEBAC's attitude toward RADECO. Over most of the life of the project, the host country remained skeptical for two reasons. First, SEEBAC was concerned that the project might be an instrument for introducing alien methodologies, and even alien content, to Dominican education, in spite of the project's firm commitments to adhere to the established Dominican curriculum. Such a response to innovations proposed by outsiders is neither uncommon nor surprising. The general lesson here for technical advisors (TAs) is the importance of practicing flexibility and understanding. An international TA needs to assume a consistent posture of presenting proposed innovations as just that—proposals. The approach, in other words, is that a project is an investigative process, or an adaptive process—an exercise in learning whether a given innovation is appropriate for the context. Any suggestion that a project seeks to substitute "superior" systems for "inferior" is likely to damage lines of communication, local cooperation, and ultimately chances for institutionalization.

Second, there was local skepticism about the very notion of teaching by radio. There was nothing surprising in this either. From the beginning, the objective of the RADECO interactive radio project sequence has been to test the effectiveness of using radio not as a *supplement* to conventional instruction, but as the *principal* instructional medium. The idea was an innovation and did indeed need to be proven.

More basically though, these doubts seemed clearly to spring from a reaction instantly familiar to anyone with experience in educational technologies: the very common, almost reflexive concern about replacing teachers with machines. Characteristically, it is not teachers themselves, but administrators and union leaders who are hardest to convince of the usefulness of technological innovations in general, and instructional broadcasting in particular. Teachers are in fact dependable allies of well-made instructional broadcasts. Administrators, removed from the classroom, are more apt than teachers to cling to their preconceptions. After experiencing the usefulness of quality instruction delivered by radio, teachers are commonly pleased with the enhancements such materials bring to their work.

Teachers, moreover, are quick to perceive that the idea of a radio as an autonomous "teaching machine" is implausible and that the radio does not pose any threat to them. Radio instruction for children cannot function without the presence of a teacher or other supervising adult.

At the beginning of 1986, SEEBAC formed a task force to conduct a review of the project. In March of the same year, before the task force had completed its work (and a few months prior to general elections), SEEBAC issued a departmental order establishing the Department of Radio Education under the Educational Media Division.

The institutionalizing document called for the project to become a permanent entity prior to the end of the project's pilot phase. Essentially, it specified that the purpose of institutionalization was to continue existing services in the pilot region, to preserve project systems and methodologies, and to establish a permanent educational radio operation with broad potential applications.

WITHIN THE PROJECT: STEPS TOWARD INSTITUTIONALIZATION

Essentially, what the RADECO project staff did to help bring about institutionalization was to build a good project.

RADECO's two principal products—trained national staff and the RADECO radio lessons themselves—constitute two valuable and tangible commodities, whose value has been sustained by virtue of the institutionalization of the project.

The staff preserve in their collective experience the project's uses of the interactive radio methodologies. They can generate more materials of the same kind, revise or adapt the existing materials, and provide national or international training in interactive radio techniques for purposes of adaptation. The project staff as it stands is also a fully functional instructional radio team, capable of generating programming as needed for teacher training, for formal classroom use, for adult and distance education, and for informational and community development programming.

Similarly, institutionalization of the Barahona program preserves RADECO's unique "para-formal" community development model both for international reference and for extension of the model to new regions of the Dominican Republic.

Over the first eight months of the final project year, the project staff presented these strong face-value arguments for institutionalization repeatedly and in detail, in person and in writing, to two successive Secretaries of Education and their immediate staffs; to the administrative staff, the Planning Office, and the Educational Media Division of SEEBAC; and to the Office of the Technical Secretary to the President.

In addition, particularly over the last six months of the pilot phase, the project seized every opportunity to invite SEEBAC staff to the field to see RADECO classrooms for themselves. Perhaps the project's most passionate advocate was its constituency: the learners and their families in the RADECO communities, and in particular, the RADECO auxiliaries have had a telling effect on institutionalization simply by having received visitors. Visiting a

RADECO community to observe a radio lesson in use provided persuasive evidence of the program's worth.

BRIDGE FUNDING

The role of the USAID/Santo Domingo Mission was also important to institutionalization. USAID Santo Domingo promoted institutionalization by arranging for modest continuing funding when USAID funding ended. Under provisions of the Caribbean Basin Initiative (CBI), limited local funds generated through interest on debt-servicing revenues are sometimes available, based on Mission recommendations, for use for designated development purposes. The mission recommended that a line of funding from this source be provided for the purpose of sustaining the institutionalized project for up to one year. SEEBAC used the funds to construct an addition to the Secretariat headquarters to house RADECO offices and a studio and to supplement SEEBAC's new radio education budget.

It is important to note that these funds were not used as an inducement to institutionalize RADECO. Institutionalization was firmly in place before the availability of continuing funding was made known. The funding was a response to institutionalization, not a cause of it.

CONCLUSIONS

Host-country site selection at the beginning of a project has a great deal to do with its successful implementation in the end. In the Dominican Republic, a significant number of educators, children, and their families were warm to the project from its beginnings and have remained so. Equally important, there was a genuine need in the Dominican Republic, perceived and expressed independently by the host government, for what the project had to offer. These two basic considerations—a general atmosphere of acceptance (or at least an absence of broad-based hostility) and genuine need noted and expressed by host-country nationals themselves—ought to be considered essential in country-site selection.

Working within the education establishment—retraining SEEBAC employees to take key project responsibilities while maintaining close continuing contact with SEEBAC leadership—played a critical role in institutionalization as well, so that ultimately, RADECO became a Dominican-owned experiment.

7/Adapting RADECO to Other Countries

Applying the RADECO model in other countries will require careful adaptation. Changes in the RADECO curriculum will be needed in order to satisfy the requirements of educational authorities. The availability of airtime is another factor to take into account. In the many countries that do not have local radio stations, for instance, radio-based education would have to be carried out by national networks.

Other considerations include the geographical setting of the targeted communities and availability of personnel to serve these communities. Access to targeted communities, even if challenging, must be at least intermittently possible year round, since delivery of curriculum materials to the radio schools is essential to the success of the program. Limited numbers of good administrators, supervisors, and proctors can also be a constraining factor in developing this type of project on a cost-effective scale.

The RADECO project's cost effectiveness cannot be matched if a radio-based program does not serve a sufficient number of communities. In the Dominican Republic, the break-even* point of RADECO—where RADECO's per-

---

* The "break-even" concept, though appealing, is also somewhat

pupil costs equaled those of regular primary school—is around 100 communities per region. In other countries, the break-even point might be higher depending on the costs of mobilizing personnel to those regions and on the degree of geographical dispersion of communities within a certain region. On the other hand, if geographically dispersed communities could be served by one national broadcast, this would have a positive effect in reducing the costs of operating the program and lowering the break-even point of the number of communities per region. The trade-offs are many and must be identified in each country to formulate the most effective strategy.

A Replication Case Study: RADECO's Use of Nicaragua Radio Math

Replication or adaptation can mean any of several things: introducing an established system or methodology to a new host country where such systems are not in use, rewriting and re-recording existing materials for use in another cultural setting or in a different host country, or extensively modifying existing materials for use in some very different context. In designing RADECO, replication occurred in all three senses.

RADECO introduced interactive radio to the Dominican Republic. Although the term "interactive radio" had not been coined when the project began, interactive radio was already in use, having been developed in Nicaragua and adapted in Kenya.

RADECO added little to the interactive-radio collection of instructional broadcast design techniques. The RA-

---

misleading since a RADECO model project is aimed at populations whose poverty and remoteness make provision of regular primary schools more difficult and expensive than an average school.

DECO project was innovative in its instructional design or "Master Plan," which was used for the first three years of *Letras* (see chapter three), and in RADECO's community development or "outreach" system (see chapter two).

The first- and second-grade math lessons were based closely on the Radio Mathematics/Nicaragua (RMN) production scripts and lesson outlines. The replications were carried out by a team of three full-time scriptwriters. All were veteran teachers with backgrounds in mathematics education and were trained as scriptwriters under the project.

During these first two years, changes in the RMN originals were made mostly for the sake of cultural appropriateness. The RADECO team considered some of the narrative and dramatic material in the RMN scripts inappropriate for use in the Dominican Republic and cut or replaced it accordingly. Character names were changed, the continuing cast of characters reduced, and new music written and recorded for use with the RADECO lessons.

RADECO's math lessons followed the RMN model closely over the first two years of the curriculum. The length of each lesson (a half hour), and the number of lessons in a year (170) were the same in both projects—an important practical consideration for purposes of replication. Matching lesson length and numbers makes the work of replication much easier at the design stage.

By the third and fourth years, however, the Dominican school curriculum and the RMN originals had begun to diverge notably. The divergence was not a matter of content or presentation, but simply the *pace* of presentation—the Dominican team found that the national curriculum went a little faster than the Nicaraguan originals.

Beginning in the middle of the third year, and continuing throughout the fourth, the RADECO lesson-outline writer worked directly from the Dominican national curriculum outline, much like a standard textbook writer, rather than working from the RMN material. The team still referred to the RMN scripts and took passages from the scripts when they were useful, but by this point their usefulness was decreasing steadily. Sometime during the third year was the point when the project began to generate "replications" in the third sense—increasingly divergent *adaptations* of RMN material, until finally, by year four, little script-by-script similarity remained.

Adaptation or Replication of the RADECO Model

The notion of "plug-in" replications of lessons that can be transferred easily from one nation to another was initially an ideal in the interactive-radio project sequence, but has long since proven unrealistic. That is not to say that replication itself is fictive, but simply that replication is likely to require more adaptation than was imagined initially.

To date the Radio Mathematics/Nicaragua lessons are the only interactive-radio materials that have enjoyed several successful replications, apparently in large part because of the subject's universality. There is a worldwide consistency in the processes by which mathematics is taught that no other subject in the core curriculum enjoys. Reading and language arts are language-specific. No basic reading text, and little language arts instruction, is amenable to direct transfer to another language. Even when countries share the same language, dialectical differences may make it difficult to utilize reading and language lessons without modification. Social studies material is often too subjective and culture-specific to be transferable. Elementary science material may prove to be more directly replicable, but as of this writing interactive-radio lessons in science are not yet at hand.

REPLICATING THE RADECO LESSONS

So what does replication really mean? Specific elements in the array of standard interactive-radio instructional patterns can be replicated, such as question-and-answer formulae, drill-and-practice devices, and individual-response cues. Replication project staff can learn these techniques by studying interactive-radio production scripts in other content areas or by studying translated scripts.

Instructional design is often replicable. The Master Plan used in designing the curriculum for RADECO consisted of a morphemic/graphemic order of presentation, out of which scriptwriters constructed pre-reading and decoding exercises, and later, basic reading text. Many of the decoding exercises in grades one and two probably could be used intact. Some of the later basic text could also be used intact or with modifications as needed for cultural and dialectical variations.

The "Master Plan" was developed as a device for teaching basic decoding skills to Spanish-speaking beginning readers. It was written with the morphophonemic characteristics of Spanish very clearly in mind and was never intended for teaching reading in any language other than Spanish. However, given scrupulous script review, sizable amounts of script text should be replicable, or even reproducible intact.

In adapting the RADECO lessons, a replication team would probably work with three documents: a RADECO production script, the corresponding lesson outline, and the corresponding student worksheet. Using these three documents, a lesson designer could review the script page by page and segment by segment, making decisions on what material to keep, what to modify, and what original materials would need to be created.

In the case of the reading material, many of the first grade lessons might be usable nearly intact; however, progressivly more rewriting or new material will be required for the second and third grades. The team can anticipate that little of the social science and other material will be replicable, although these materials could be reviewed in any case for usable text or simply for interesting methodology.

THE FUTURE OF RADIO EDUCATION

The key to successful replication will be well-planned adaptation of the model to meet local needs and to conform to local administrative procedures. Institutions interested in using the RADECO model will need to (1) make a commitment to the basic tenets of the model—the establishment and operation of a precise, schedule-oriented production system; (2) provide the quality human resources and basic materials and equipment that the model demands; (3) assure access to the required radio time; (4) distribute learning materials in a timely manner; and (5) make provisions for regular supervision, evaluation, and support of the schools and communities being served.

The RADECO model can be used in formal schools as well as to substitute for formal schools. In formal schools, trained teachers can utilize the RADECO math or language lessons as reinforcement for their regular classes. The RADECO lessons can help teachers keep pace with curriculum requirements.

The continuity of the radio school communities developed in Barahona and the relatively high retention rates of the students served by RADECO are encouraging signs of the ability of these isolated communities to respond to new opportunities.

Replication of interactive radio materials is more than plausible; it is a likely and exciting prospect. Each replication project will be a unique experience, but that is not to say that the hopeful early notions about replicability of interactive-radio material were wrong. On the contrary, the original hopes that replications could be efficient, cost effective, and instructionally sound appear to be reasonable.

INTERNATIONAL EDUCATION UPDATE: RADIO COMMUNITY EDUCATION

Following completion of the experimental stage of the RADECO project in late 1986, the government of the Dominican Republic allocated funding to construct a new wing onto the ministry's headquarters as permanent housing for RADECO staff. On September 5, 1987, Dominican Republic Minister of Education Pedro Pichardo dedicated the radio studio and office suite built for the now institutionalized Radio Community Education (RADECO) program.

Minister Pichardo cited RADECO's target audience as the DR's numerous communities whose sparse populations make school construction difficult. "It's there where the intelligent response is the rational use of communications media; it is where RADECO appears to confront the problem," he said. Pichardo expressed confidence that the program would be expanded to cover the entire country.

SEMESTER DATE DUE			
APR 29 1993			